WORLD

OF

COLORS

EUROPE

Made in the USA (All Rights Reserved)

World of Colors Europe

WORLDOFCOLORSART@GMAIL.COM

USA

Table of Content

Choose from our fabulous selection of cities in Spain, France or Italy. Color scenes from your favorite sites around Europe!

Introduction

Table of Content, Thank You …………………………………………………………… 2-5

Spain

Seville, Zaragoza, Cordova, Barcelona, Madrid, Granada …………… 6-27

France

Paris, Eiffel Tower, Cleopatra's Needle …………………………………………… 28-31

Italy

Rome, Colosseum …………………………………………………………………………… 32-33

Family Appreciation, Conclusion, Coming Soon …………………… 32-35

WHO WE ARE

Our mission

To travel the globe in search of the best professional photos and create them into your own personal coloring art book!

The team

Skip, Zahir, Andre Edwards

Get to know your creative side and explore the world! Here are some fun images you can color to relieve stress, expand your mind or redraw your favorite city.

Thank You Family

The purpose of World of Colors artwork is to stimulate our reading family's creative juices through coloring.   We have made a compliation of images that were taken from all around Europe and transformed into a coloring extravaganza!!!   These images include   sites ranging from Paris to Barcelona and Rome.

The aim of this project is to relieve anxiety, awaken your inner traveler, and give the world color by your own hands!   The World of Colors team has provided short descriptions to go along with each image.   Allowing YOU our reading family to color the site in splitting image or recreate it with your own unique spin.

This series was made with LOVE and PASSION!!!   We hope you enjoy coloring and traveling with us as much as we enjoyed creating the project.   We TRULY   do appreciate your support; now it's time to enjoy everything from street art in Barcelona to an ancient Nubian Obelisk in Paris.

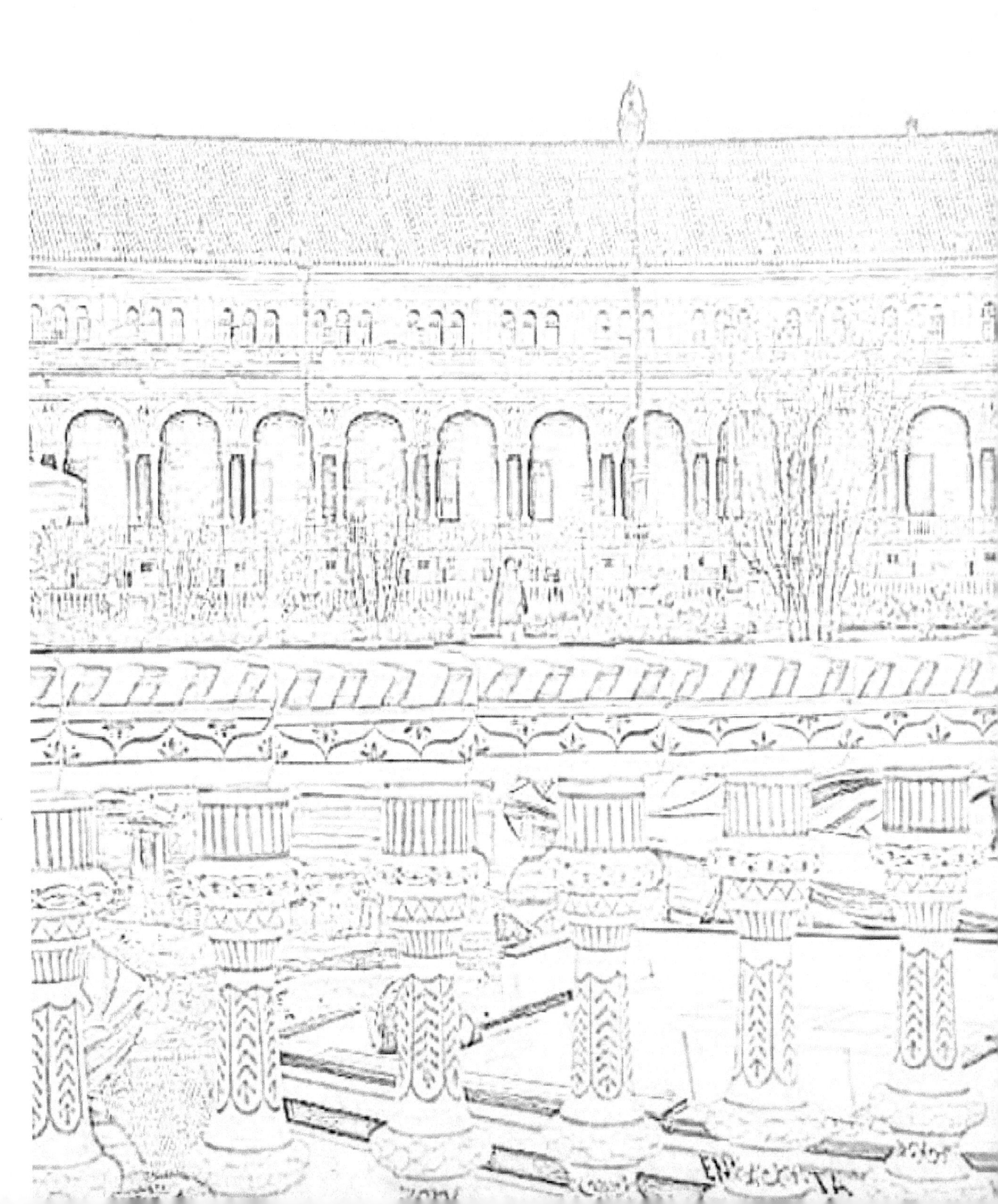

Spain {Seville}

The Plaza de Espana meaning "Spain Square" is located in Seville, Spain.   It's a landmark that reveals the countries history in religon, war and architecture ranging from the Moorish Empires to the Spainish reconquista.

Seville {Spain}

This design is located at Alcazar of Seville - Also known as "Reales Alcazar de Sevilla" or "Royal Alcazar of Seville" is a royal palace built by the Moorish Empire Umayyad.

Granada {Spain}

This Islamic art design is located inside Al Alhambra in Granada, Spain. Bright Yellow, Purple and Red color schemes shine bright on the polished marbel walls.

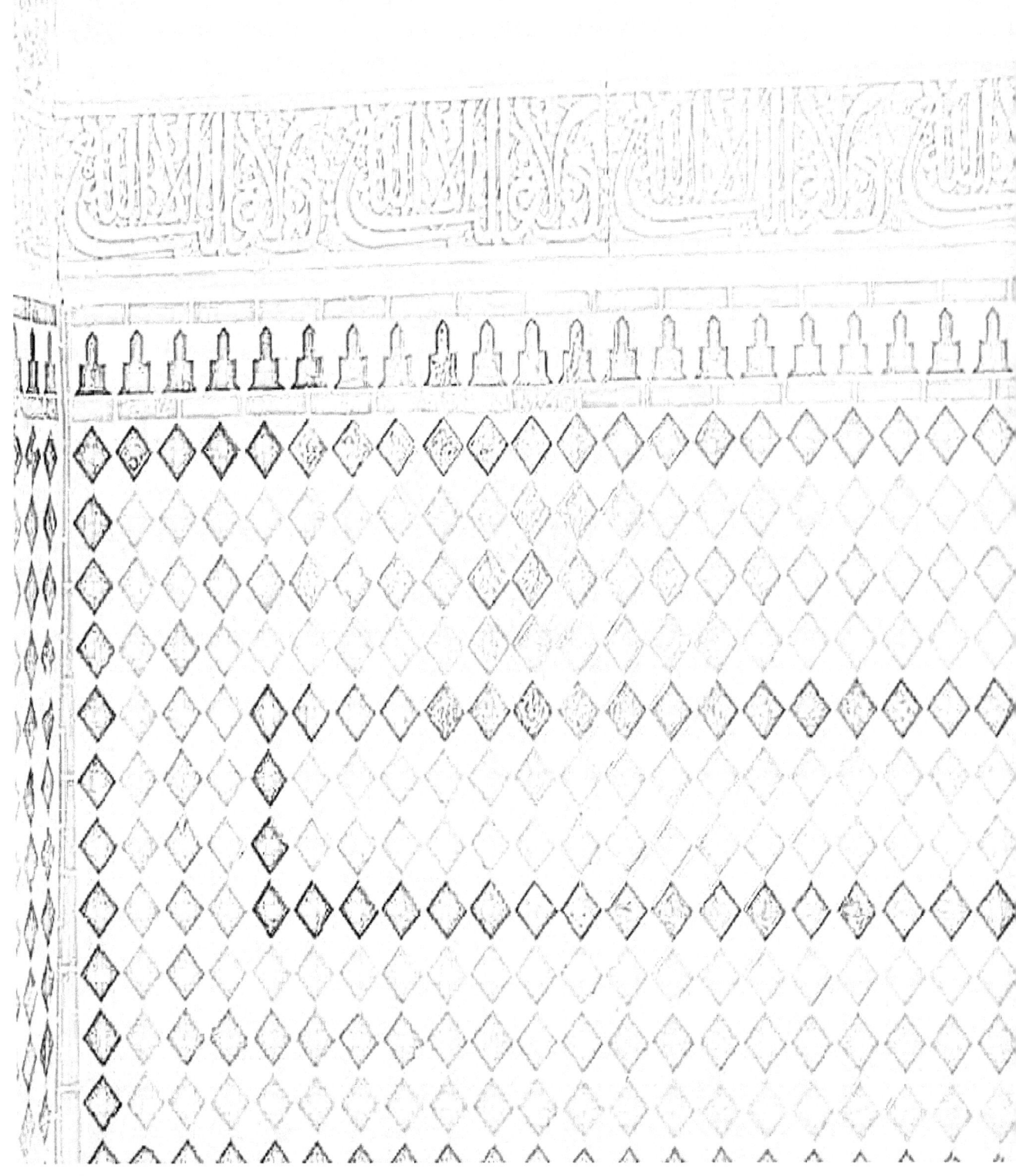

Granada {Spain}

The phrase "God is the only victor" is repeated throughout the General Life section of the Al Alhambra.

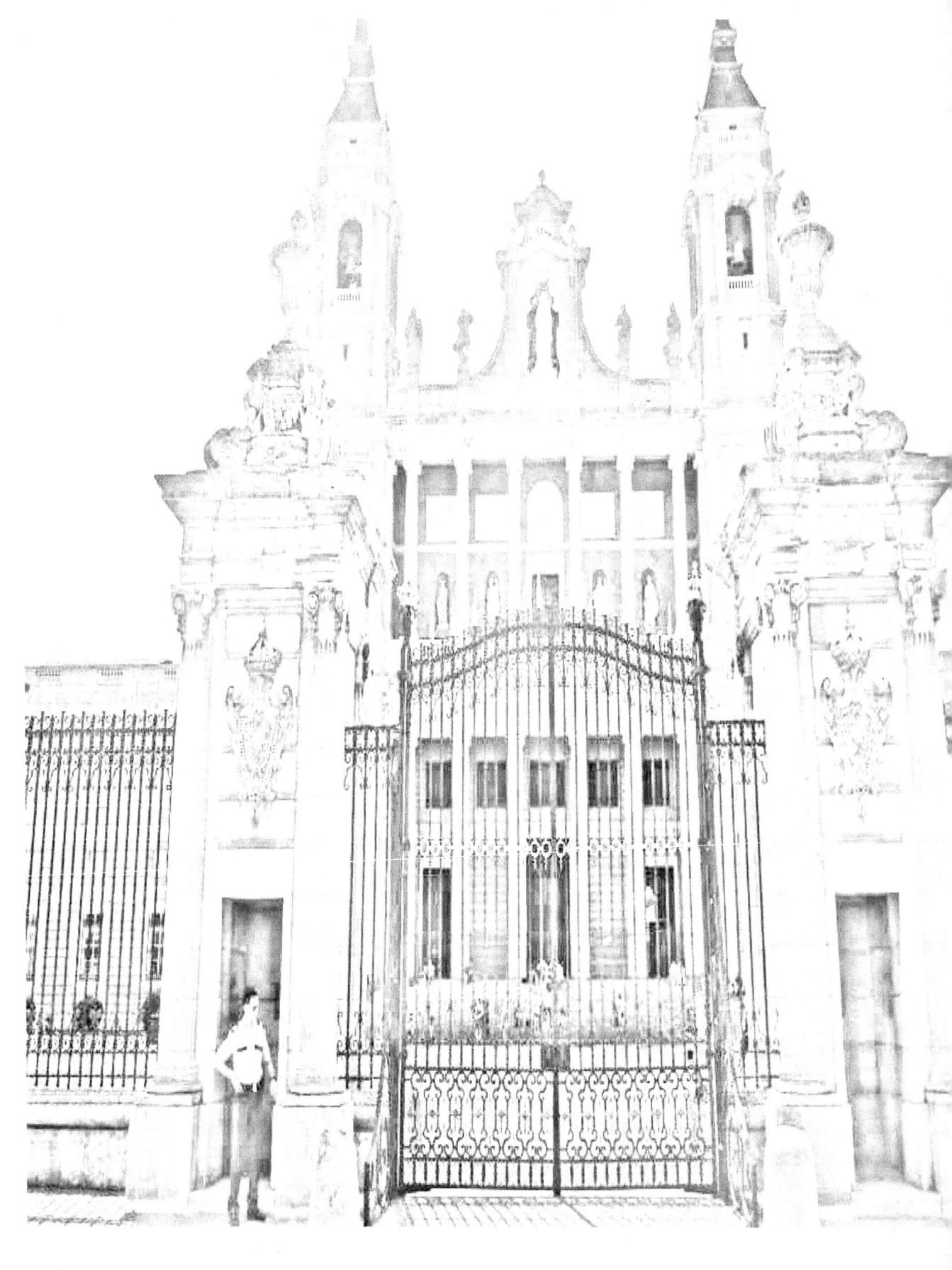

Madrid {Spain}

The Royal Palace of Madrid was built on old Moorish ruins from the Toledo Empire.   Reconstructed by King Henry III to repair damages from war as well as reflect the European renaissence.

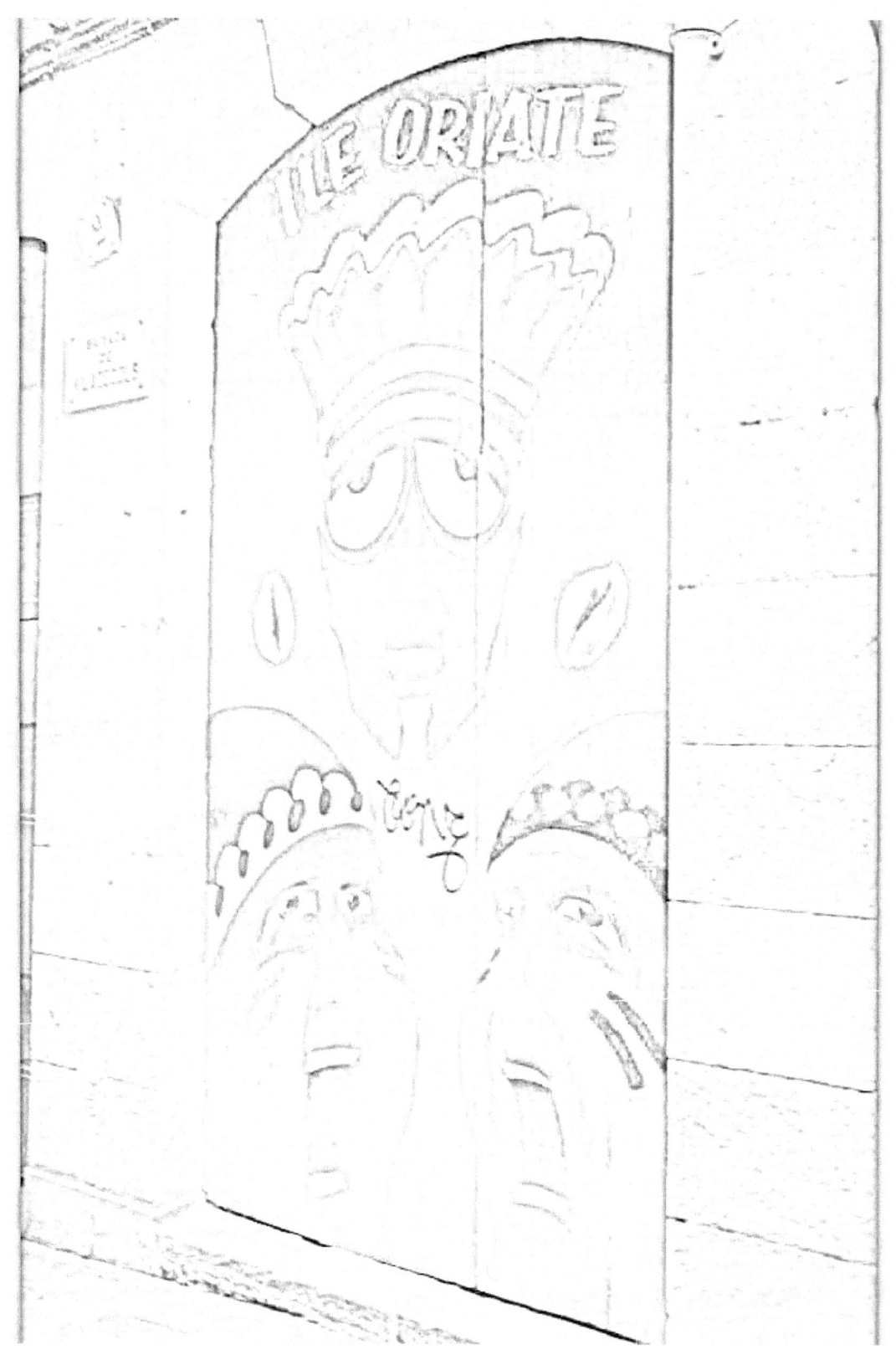

Barcelona {Spain}

Barcelona has the perfect blend of classical European and street art.   This painting resembling Native American culture is known as "The 3 Moreno's" located near the city centre.

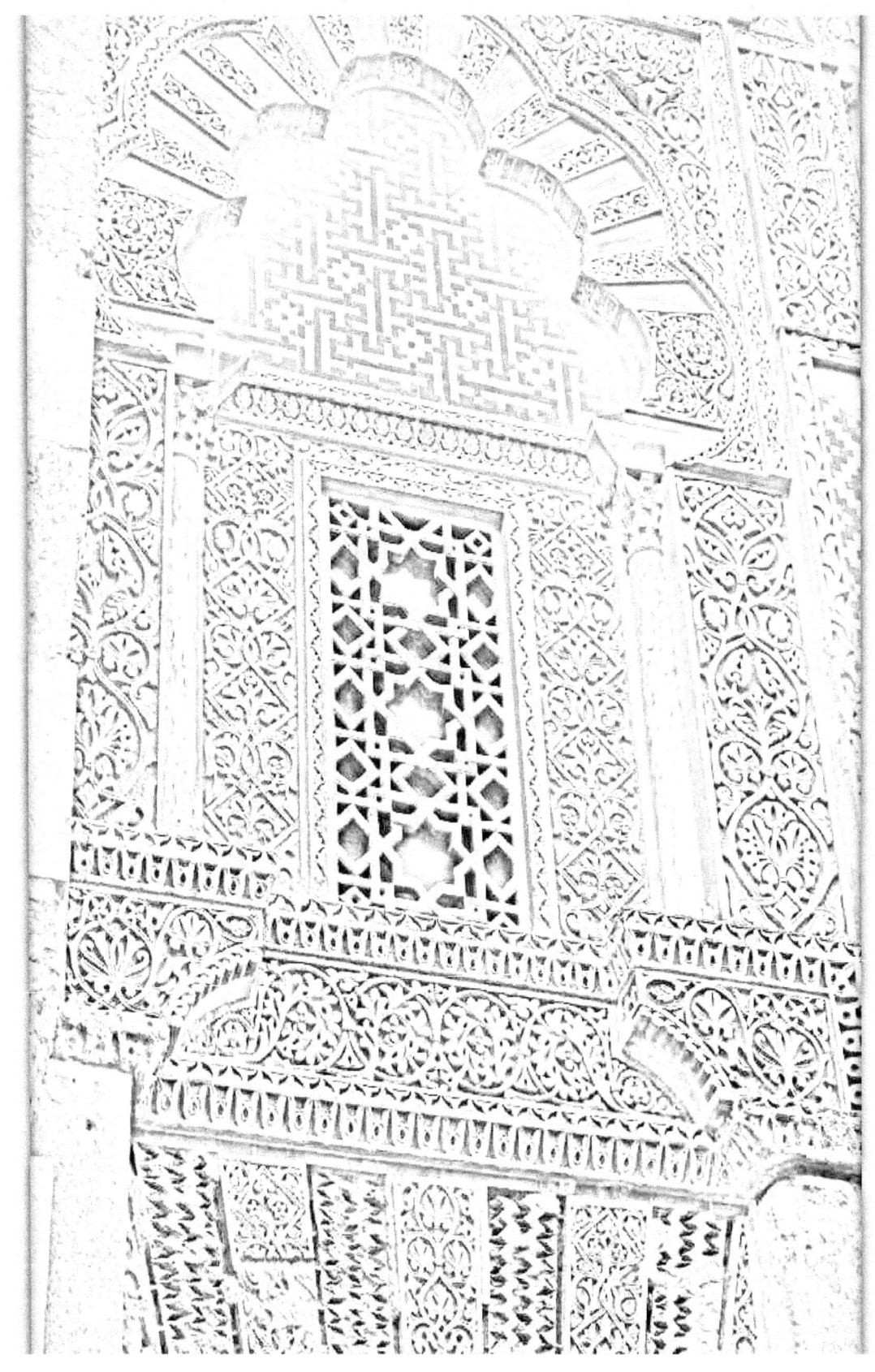

Cordova {Spain}

The Mosque-Cathedral of Cordoba is credited for being the first place for Christian and Islamic joint worship. It's gold and clay (red) exterior house thousands of years of culture and tradition .

Cordova {Spain}

Perfect symmetry is on display in every room of the Grand Mosque-Cathedral in Cordova, Spain.   Royal blue, solid gold and chestnut red blend together beautifully in this image.

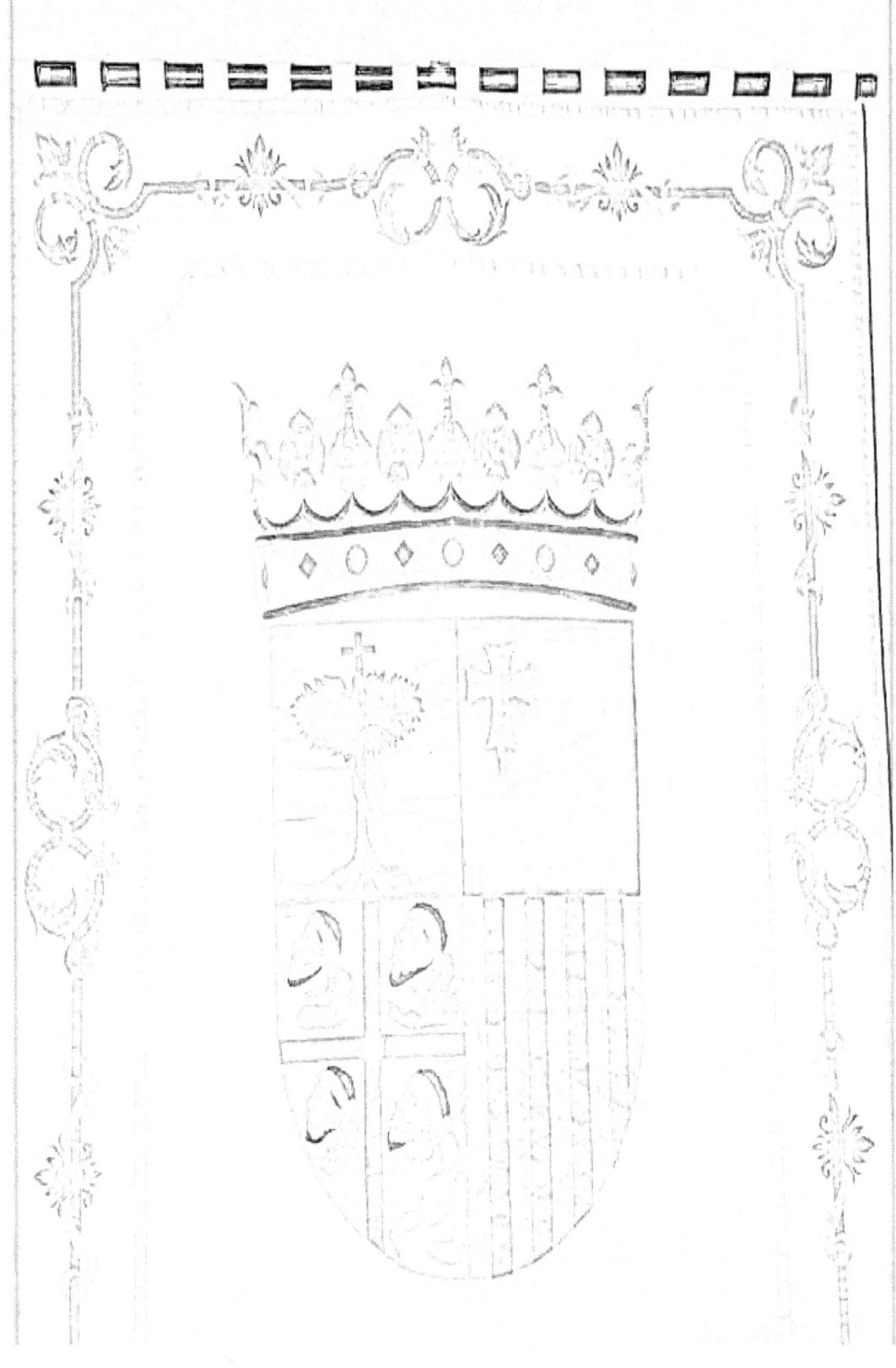

Zaragoza {Spain}

This Moorish Empire code of arms flag sits inside the Aljaferia Palace in Zaragoza Spain. The castle was built in the 11th century and later conquered by Alfonso "the battler".

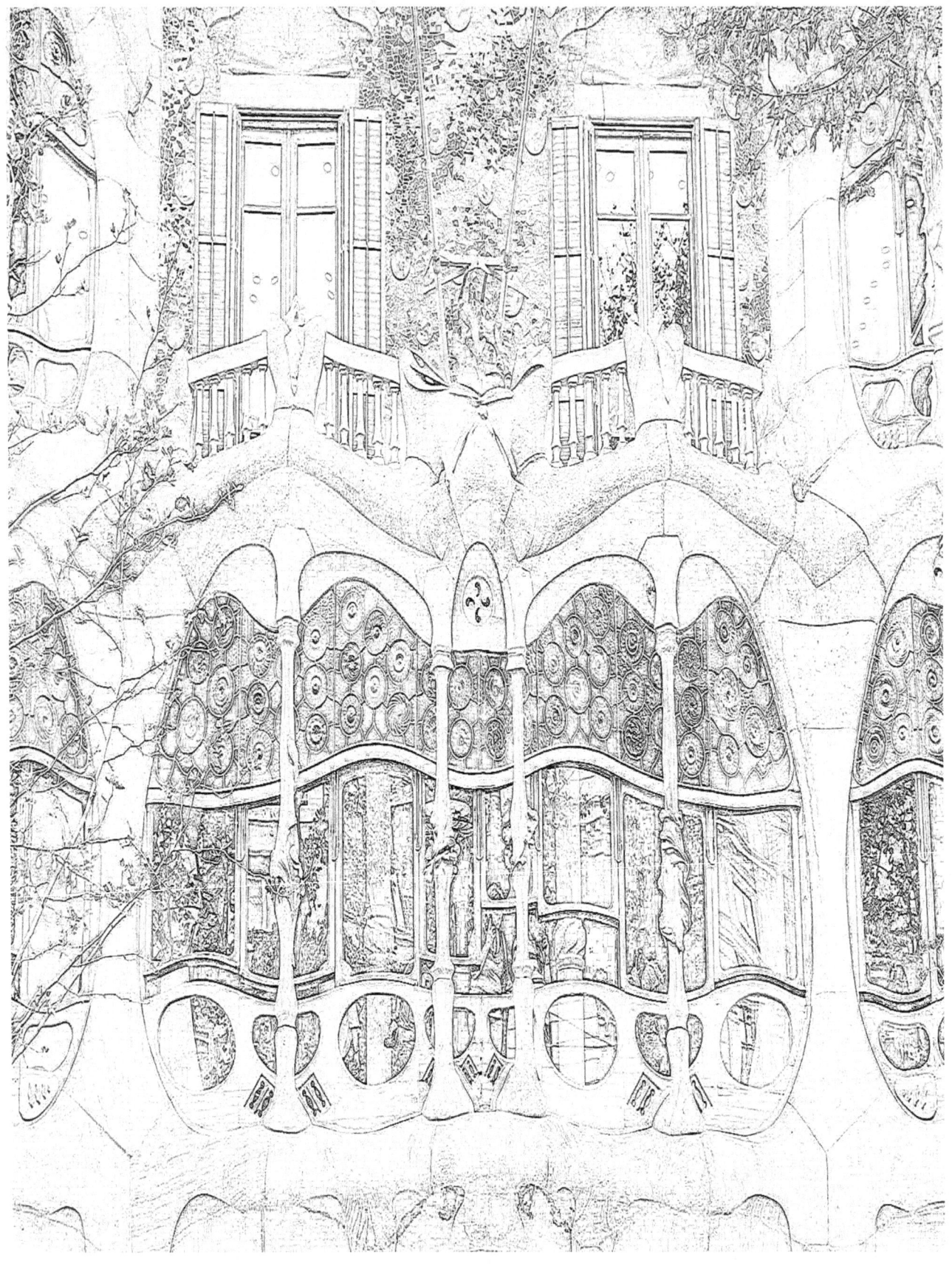

Barcelona {Spain}

The Casa Batllo or "Casa dels ossos" refered to by Catalonians means "House of Bones".   It was designed in 1904 by world famous Spainish artist Antoni Gaudi, displaying violet, tourguise and forest green flowers.

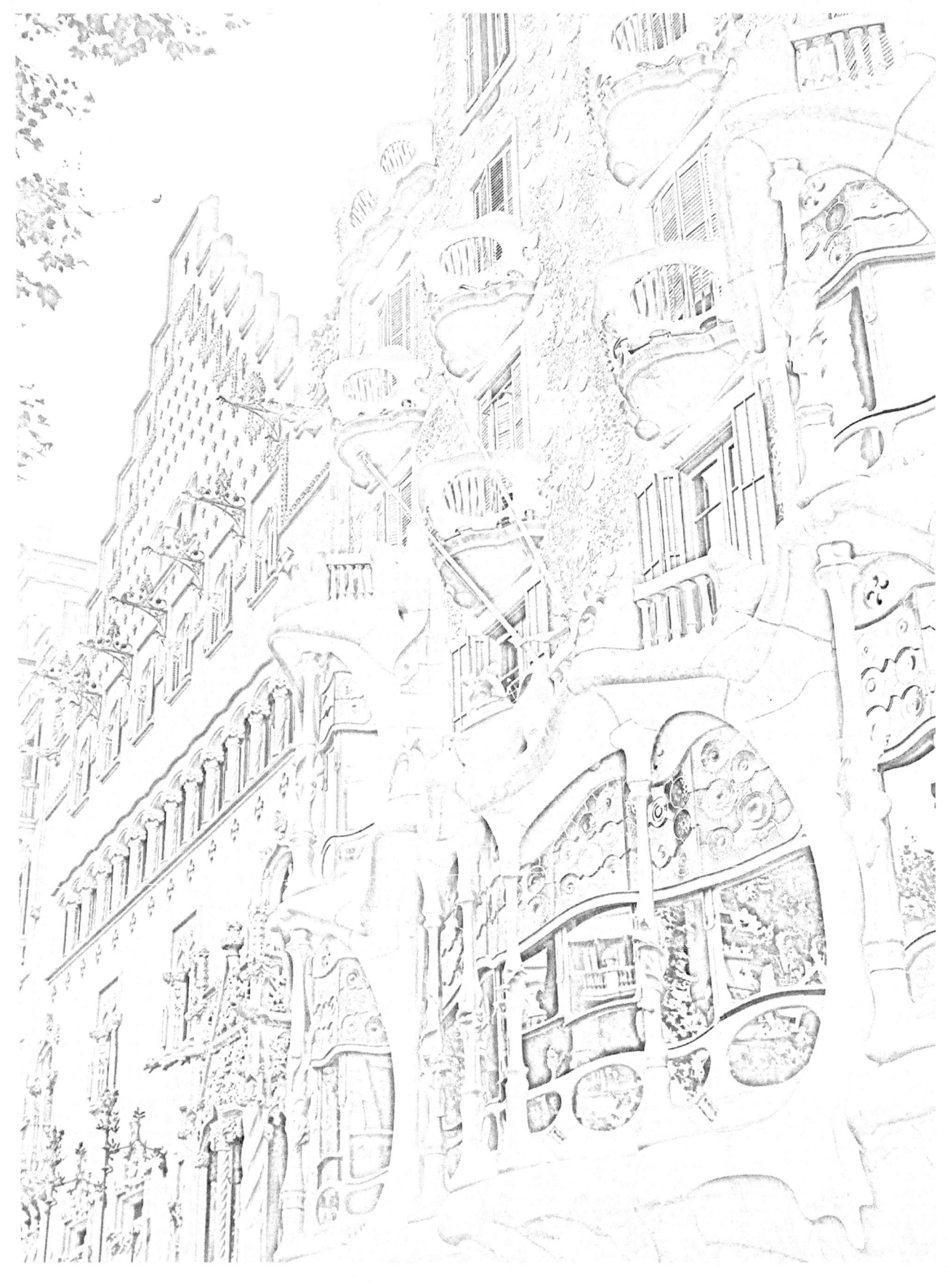

Barcelona {Spain}

Side view of Casa Batllo's lance of Saint George the patron saint of Catalonia where Barcelona's located.

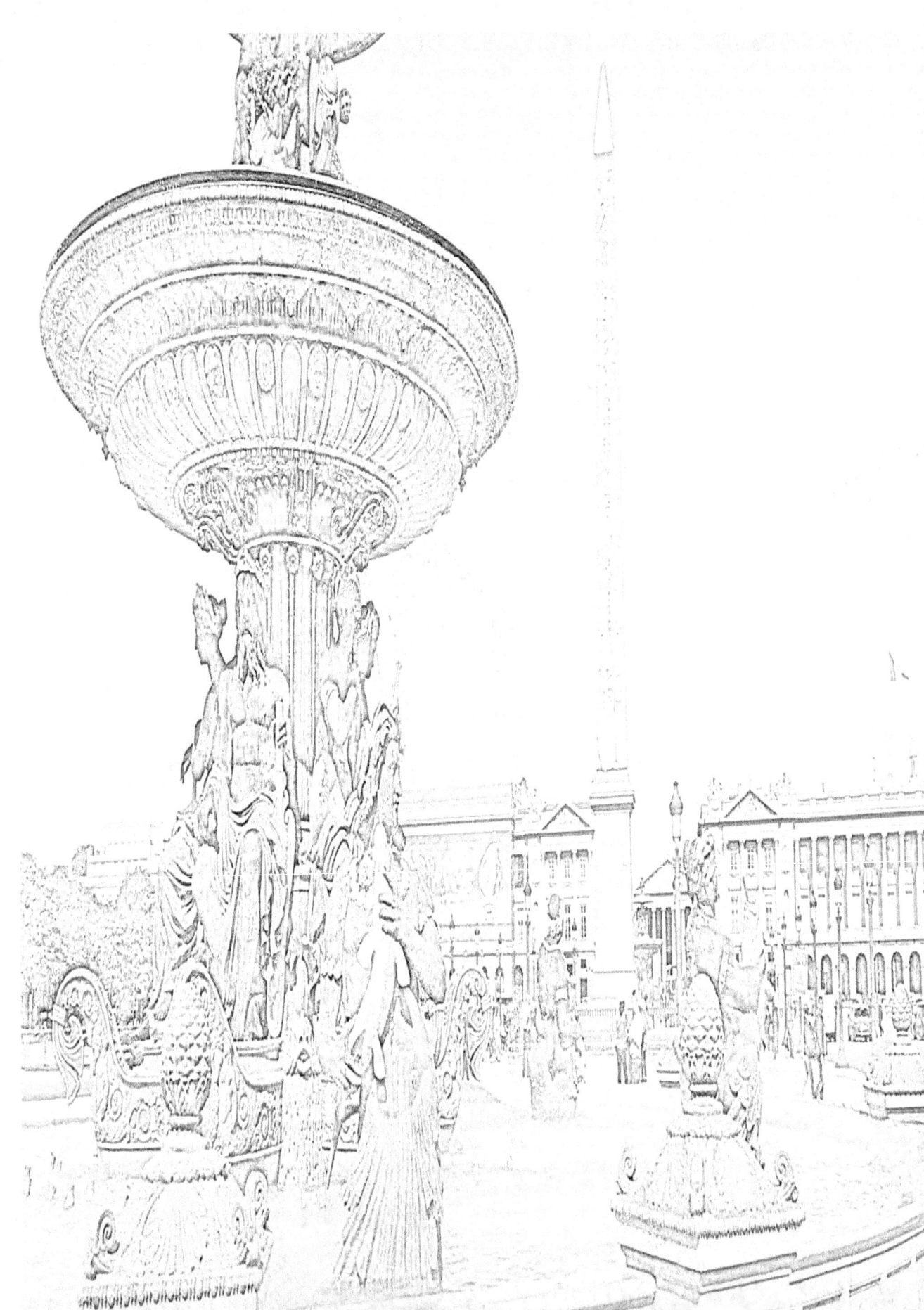

Paris {France}

Cleopatra's Needle from the Grand Luxor Temple built during the reign of King Ramsas III.   It now sits in the middle of "Place de la Concorde" in Paris France next to the gold and silver "Fontaines de la Concorde".

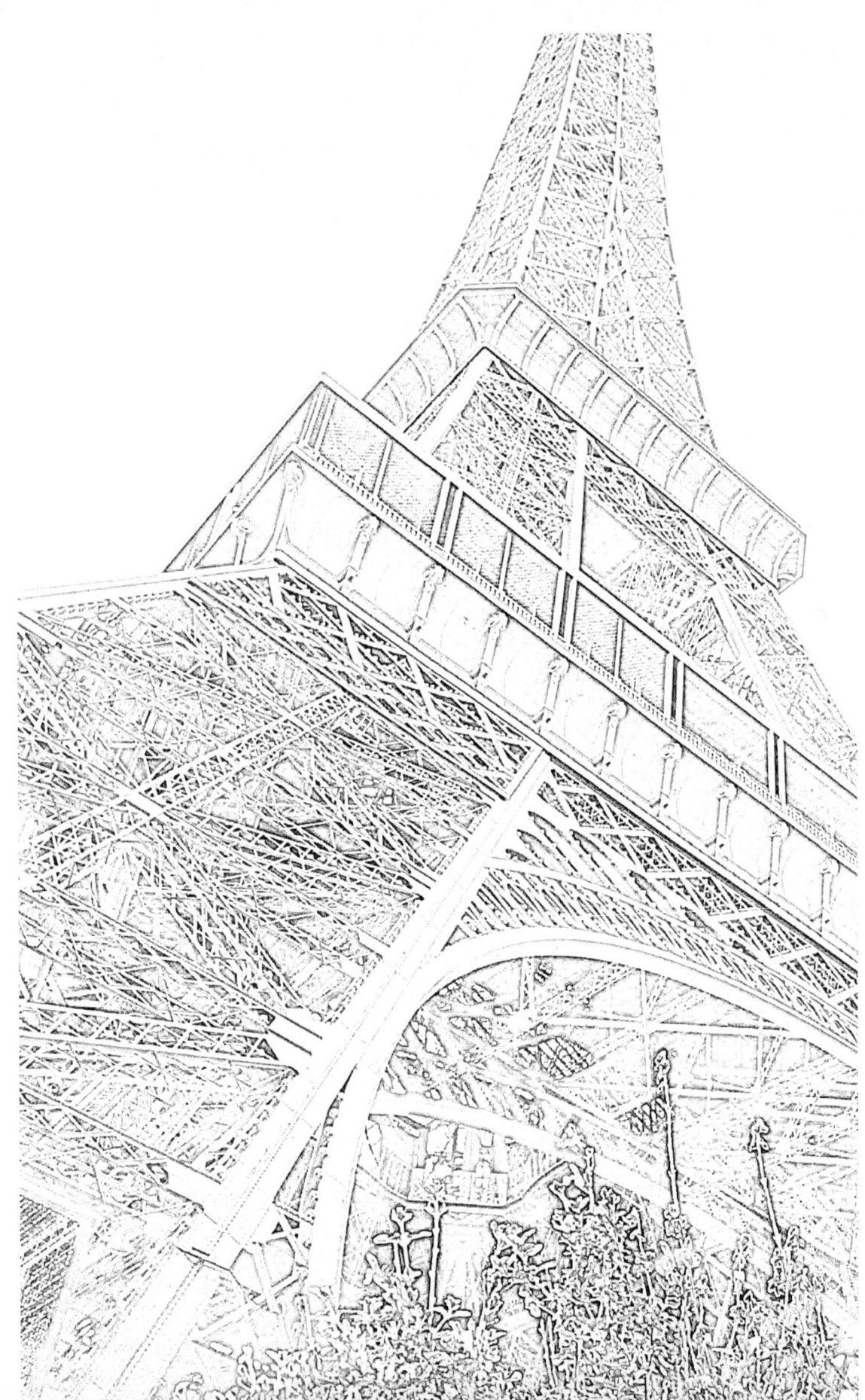

Paris {France}

The Eiffel Tower needs no introduction! The proud possession of Parisans since 1889 sits behind a bed of pink and green shrubbs.

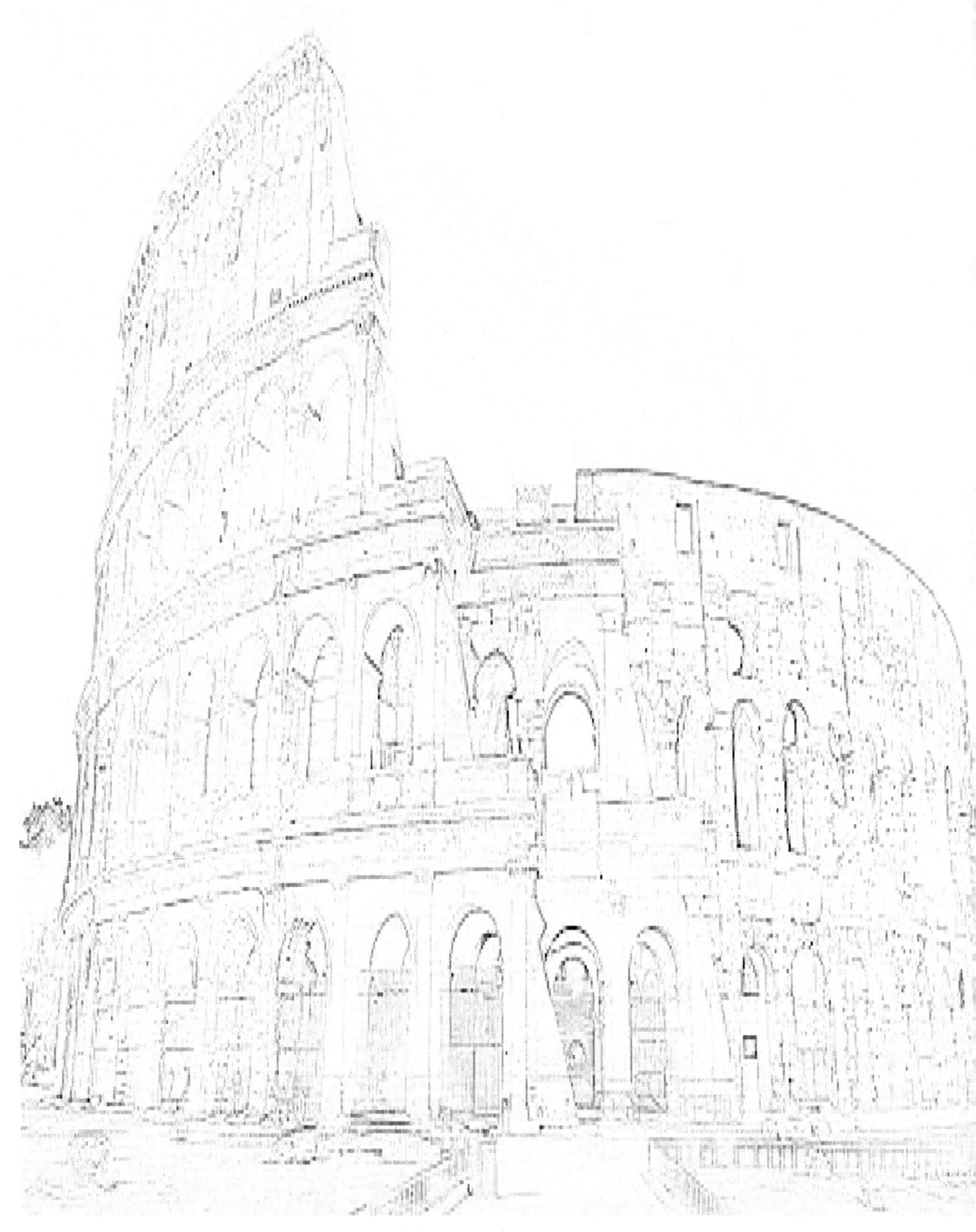

Rome {Italy}

The "Roman Colosseo" or the Flavian Amphitheatre is the largest amphitheatre in the world.   It's concrete and sand frame stands tall and remains the poster child of ancient Rome.

Family Appreciation

On behalf of the World of Colors Team we'd like to say THANK YOU for your support. You are offically apart of the World of Colors family! We look forward to sharing artistic projects with you in the future! We also encourage constant feedback at *worldofcolorsart@gmail.com* from WOC family members to continuously improve our relationship!

Conclusion

This concludes the World of Colors Europe tour!   Be on the lookout for more series from our team......

COMNG SOON......

World of Colors Asia = Fall 2017

World of Colors Africa = Winter 2018

World of Colors Kids = Spring 2018

www.ingramcontent.com/pod-product-compliance
Lightning Source LLC
Chambersburg PA
CBHW062208220526
45470CB00009B/2963